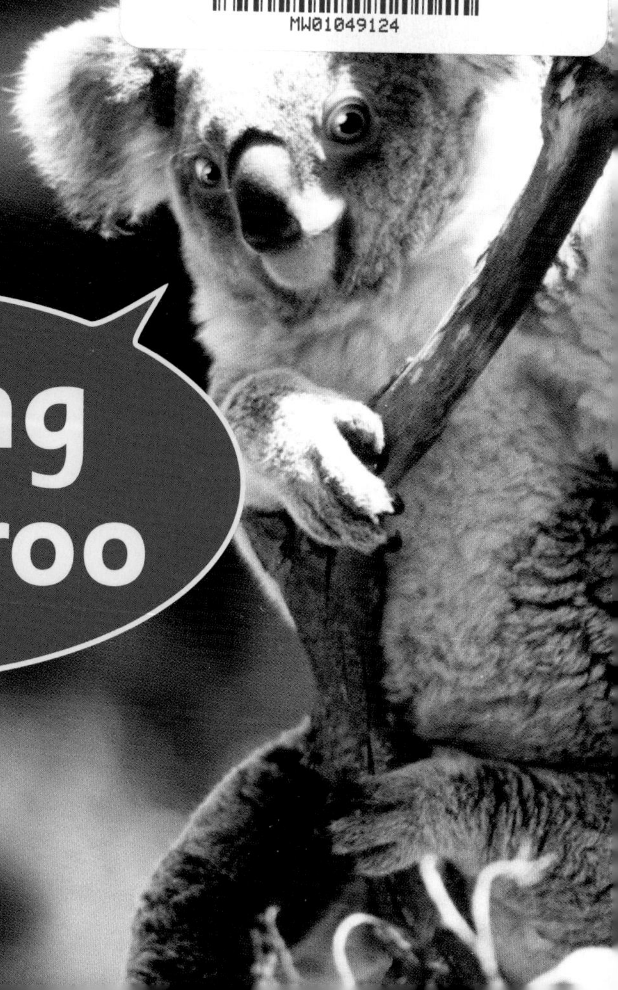

Kicking kangaroo

Words by Katy Pike
Pictures by Luke Jurevicius

Kangaroo

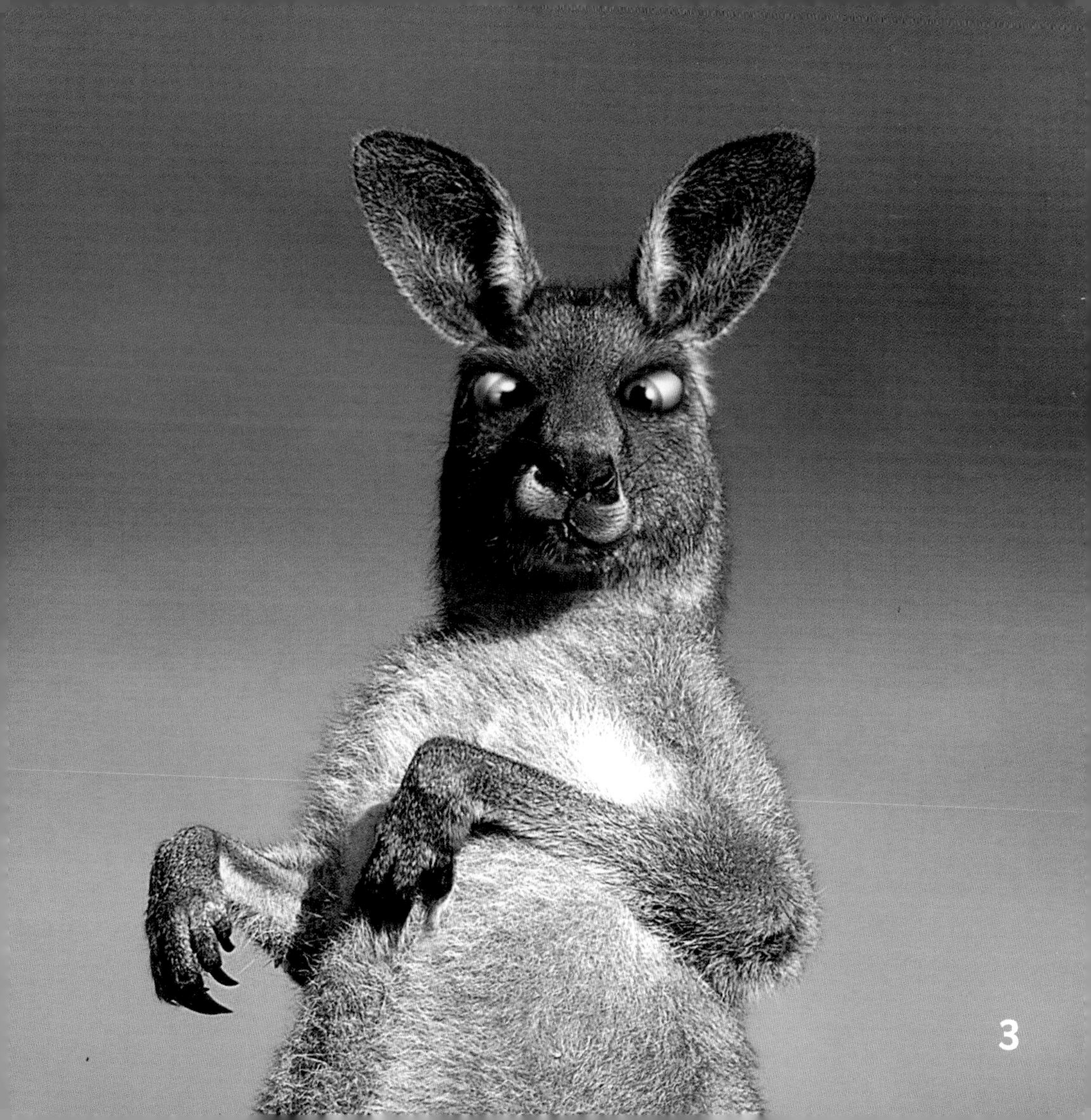

Kangaroos like
to kick.

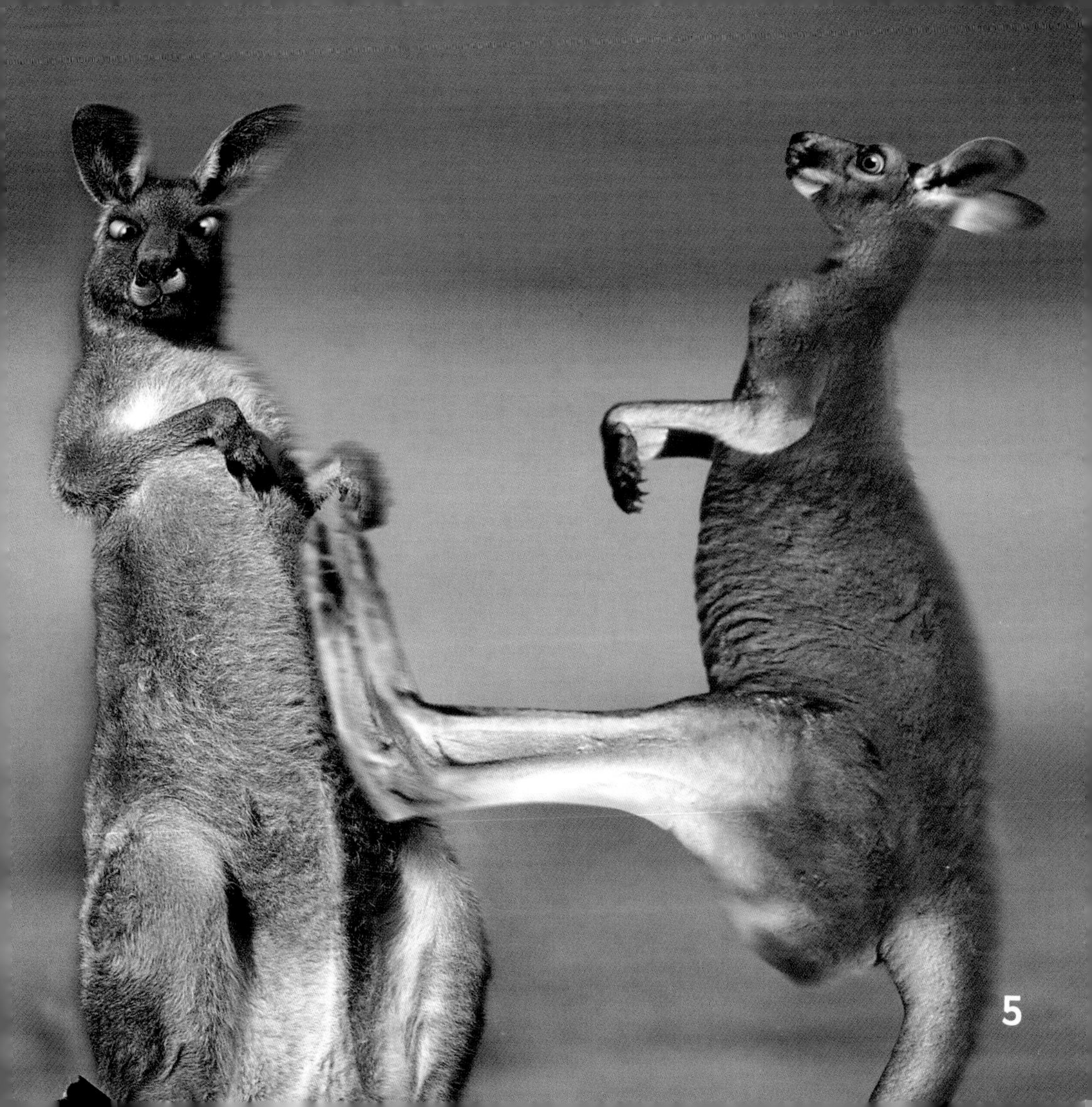

Kangaroo kicks
a king.

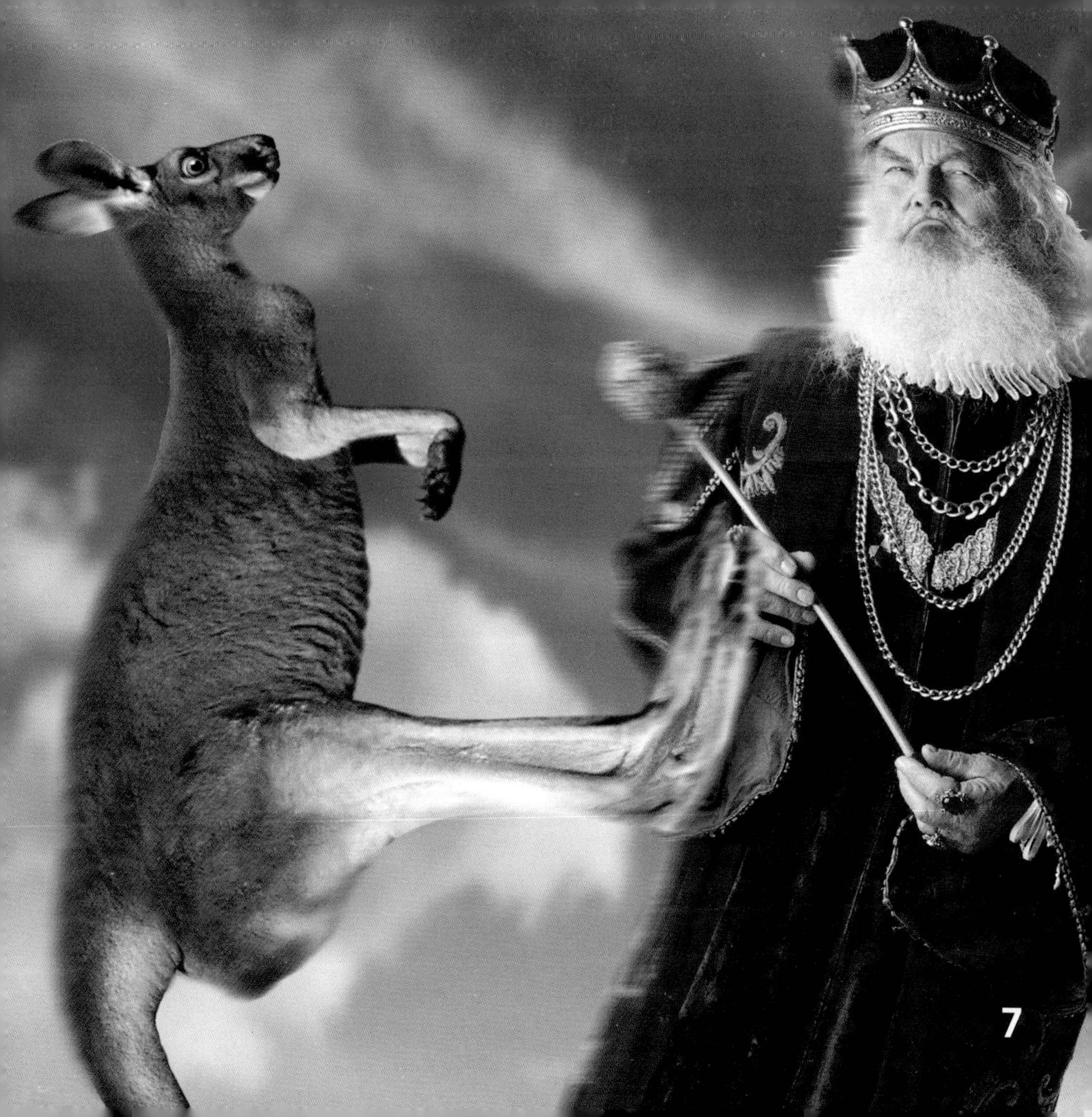

Koala

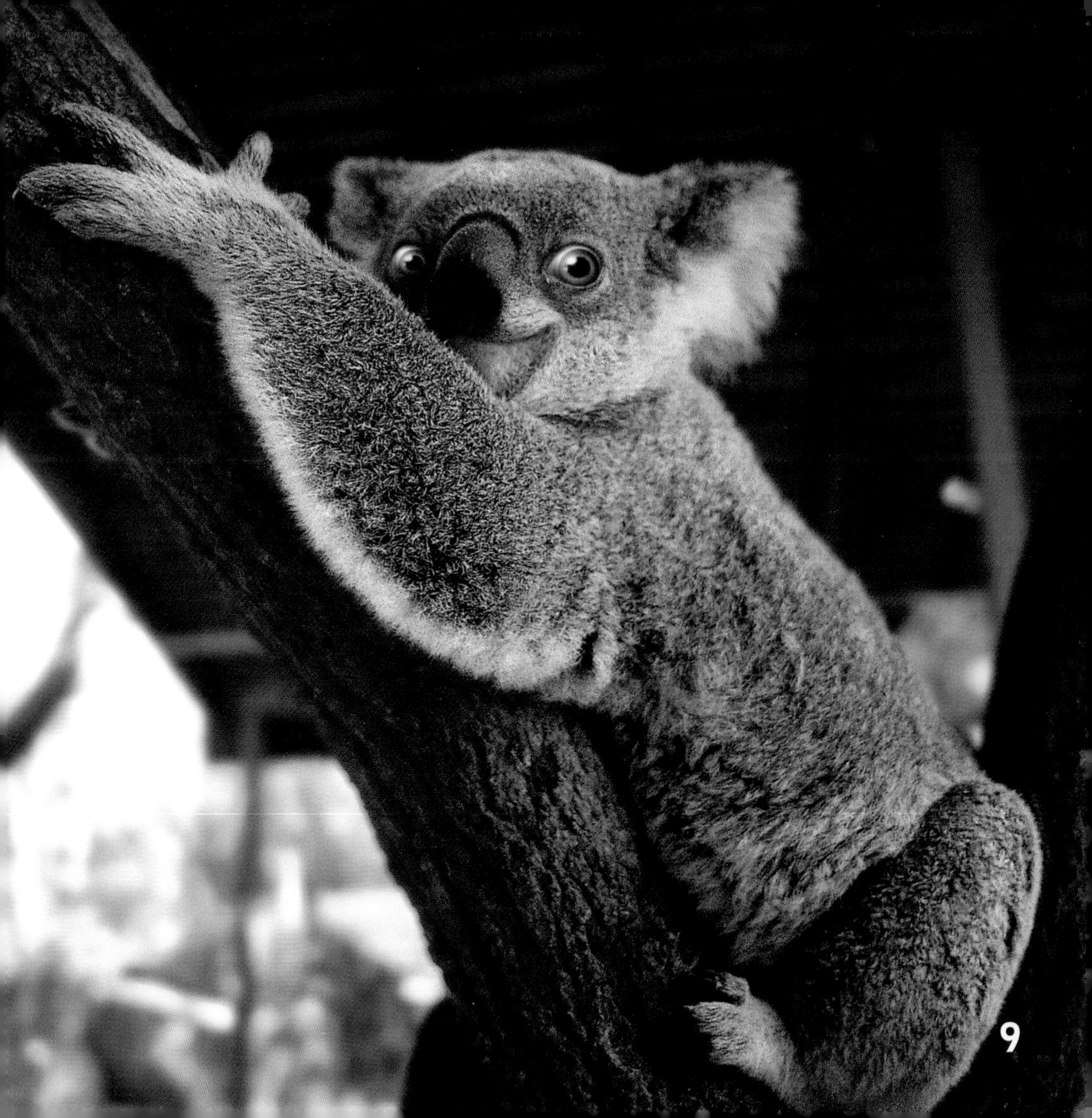

Koalas like to kiss.

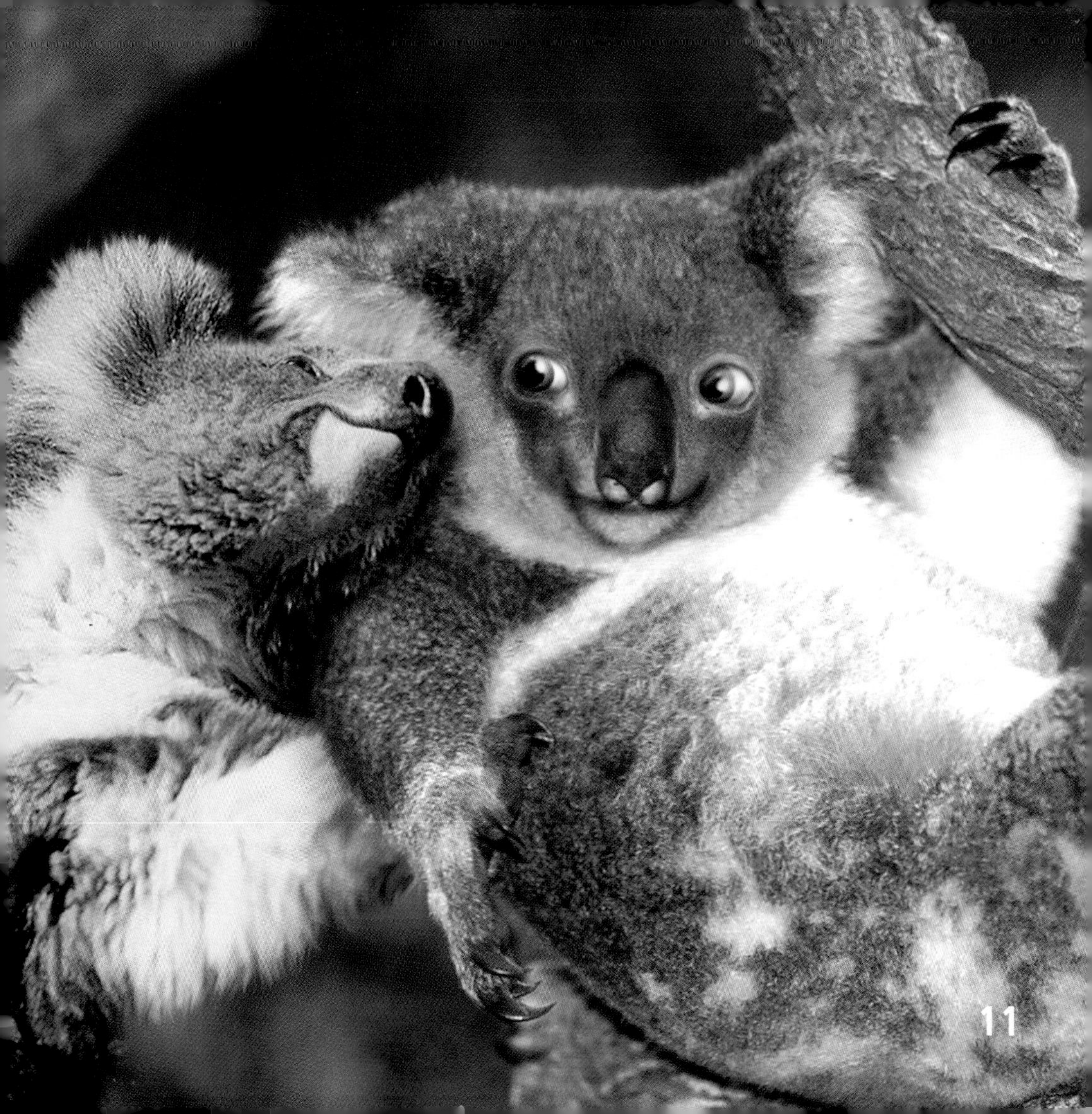

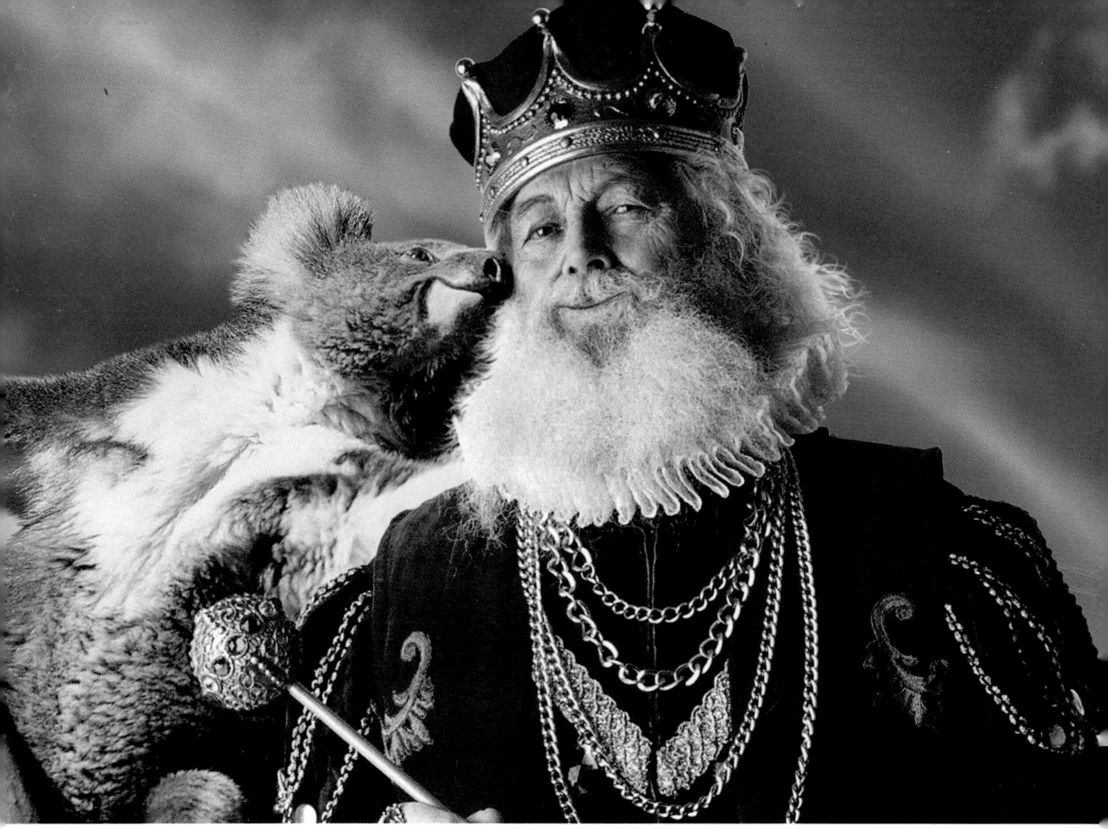

Koala kisses the king.